COMPLETE GUIDE TO MULE FARMING

Expert Techniques, Sustainable Practices, And Profitable Strategies For Successful Breeding And Care

GIOVANNI MALAKAI

DISCLAIMER

This book's content is solely intended for informational and educational purposes. The author and publisher of this book make no express or implied representations or warranties of any kind regarding the completeness, accuracy, reliability, suitability, or availability of the information, products, services, or related graphics contained in it, even though every effort has been made to ensure their accuracy and dependability. You consequently absolutely assume all risk associated with any reliance you may have on such material.

The author's own experiences and studies serve as the foundation for the techniques and procedures covered in this book. They might not be appropriate for every circumstance or person. Before putting any advice or recommendations from this book into practice, readers should use their own discretion and take into account their unique situation. Consulting with qualified professionals who specialize in veterinary care and animal management is always a good idea. Any direct, indirect, incidental or consequential damages resulting from using or relying on the material in this book are disclaimed by the author and publisher. Any decisions made by the reader based on the information presented herein are at their own risk.

TABLE OF CONTENTS

CHAPTER ONE 13

INTRODUCTION TO MULE FARMING 13

RECOGNIZING THE FUNCTION OF MULES IN AGRICULTURE.............13

ADVANTAGES OF FARMING MULES..14

ESSENTIAL TERMS FOR MULE FARMING...16

SAFETY MEASURES AND THE WELFARE OF ANIMALS 17

ORGANIZING YOUR MULE FARMING BUSINESS................................19

CHAPTER TWO 21

CHOOSING AND PURCHASING MULES...21

SELECTING THE BEST BREEDS OF MULES FOR YOUR FARM.............21

ASSESSING THE AGE AND HEALTH OF MULES................................22

BUYING MULES FROM RELIABLE VENDORS 23

MULE TRANSPORTATION AND INTRODUCTION TO YOUR FARM 24

EXAMS FOR HEALTH AND QUARANTINE FOR NEW MULES 26

CHAPTER THREE 27

MULE HOUSING AND AMENITIES...27

CREATING APPROPRIATE STABLES AND BARNS 27

OPTIONS FOR MULE ENCLOSURE FENCING 28

SYSTEMS FOR WATERING AND FEEDING 29

ORGANIZING AND MAINTAINING SPACES 31

PUTTING WASTE MANAGEMENT PRACTICES INTO PRACTICE 32

CHAPTER FOUR 35

CONSUMPTION AND MEDICAL CARE..35

RECOGNIZING THE NUTRITIOUS NEEDS OF MULES 35

MAKING WELL-BALANCED MEALS FOR MULES...................................36

HEALTH CARE PREVENTIVE MEASURES.......................................37

COMMON HEALTH PROBLEMS AND SOLUTIONS FOR MULES..........38

COLLABORATING WITH FARRIERS AND VETERINARIANS..................39

CHAPTER FIVE...41

MULE HANDLING AND TRAINING 41

DEVELOPING RELATIONSHIPS AND TRUST WITH MULES..................41

FUNDAMENTAL TRAINING METHODS FOR MULE HANDLING 42

INSTRUCTING IN SIGNALS AND COMMANDS....................................43

MANAGING DIFFICULTIES AND BEHAVIORAL PROBLEMS.................44

ADVANCED INSTRUCTION FOR OPERATIONAL MULES 46

CHAPTER SIX...47

BREEDING AND REPRODUCTION OF MULES 47

KNOWING THE BIOLOGY OF MULE REPRODUCTION 47

CHOOSING BREEDING STOCK..48

BREEDING STRATEGIES AND SCHEDULE...50

MULE PREGNANCY TREATMENT 51

HANDLING AND TAKING CARE OF FOALS...52

CHAPTER SEVEN 55

USING MULES IN AGRICULTURE...55

MULES' FUNCTIONS IN AGRICULTURE 55

PREPARING MULES FOR PARTICULAR TASKS 56

MULE EQUIPMENT AND HARNESSING...57

PRECAUTIONARY STEPS FOR FARM WORK SAFETY...........................58

OPTIMIZING PRODUCTIVITY WITH MULE TEAMS 59

CHAPTER EIGHT 61

MULE WELL-BEING AND ILLNESS CONTROL...................61

PRACTICES FOR PREVENTIVE HEALTH 61

IDENTIFYING SYMPTOMS OF DISEASE OR INJURY 62

INITIAL CARE FOR HORSES 64

IMMUNIZATION AND DISEASE PREVENTION 65

PLANNING FOR EMERGENCY REACTIONS 66

CHAPTER NINE 69

PLANNING AND MANAGEMENT OF FINANCES 69

SETTING A BUDGET FOR MULE FARMING ACTIVITIES........69

SOURCES OF INCOME FOR MULE FARMING 70

MAINTAINING DOCUMENTS AND ANALYZING FINANCES 72

RISK MANAGEMENT AND INSURANCE............................73

STRATEGIES FOR LONG-TERM SUSTAINABILITY 74

CHAPTER TEN 77

PROMOTING PRODUCTS AND MULES.............................77

PUTTING YOUR MULE FARM'S BRANDING TO USE 77

STRATEGIES FOR PROMOTION AND ADVERTISING.............78

PROVIDING PRODUCTS AND MULES FOR SALE 80

RELATIONSHIP MANAGEMENT WITH CUSTOMERS 81

INCREASING MARKET CAPABILITY................................83

CHAPTER ELEVEN 85

UPCOMING DEVELOPMENTS AND TRENDS IN MULE FARMING............85

NEW DEVELOPMENTS IN MULE FARMING TECHNOLOGIES 85

ENVIRONMENTAL IMPACT AND SUSTAINABLE PRACTICES...............86

INITIATIVES FOR EDUCATION AND TRAINING 88

INTERNATIONAL MARKET PROSPECTS 89

ADJUSTMENT TO SHIFTING MARKET CONDITIONS............................90

CHAPTER TWELVE 93

COMMON QUESTIONS AND EXTENSIVE ANSWERS 93

DISPELLING FREQUENTLY HELD MYTHS ABOUT MULE FARMING 93

SOLVING TYPICAL PROBLEMS FOR NOVICES......................................94

FREQUENTLY ASKED QUESTIONS CONCERNING FARMING 95

RESOURCES FOR ADDITIONAL EDUCATION AND ASSISTANCE...........96

GETTING IN TOUCH WITH COMMUNITIES THAT FARM MULES.........97

ABOUT THE BOOK

Anyone interested in mule farming can use this book, "Complete Guide to Mule Farming," as a complete reference. It starts by going over the essentials of comprehending mules' function in farming and stressing the many advantages they offer to farming operations. The book provides readers with a strong foundation of knowledge by introducing them to key terms in mule husbandry. The emphasis on safety measures and animal welfare requirements sets a reasonable standard for handling mules on the farm.

The choice and purchase of mules is one of the main topics discussed. The right mule breeds for each reader's unique farm demands will be revealed, along with how to assess the health and age of mule purchases and make well-informed decisions from reliable sources. Along with instructions on quarantine protocols and health examinations for recently arrived mules, the book also offers advice on moving and acclimating mules to the farm.

Mule housing and facilities are important farm management considerations, and this book provides advice on how to build appropriate barns and stables, choose fencing, put in place watering and feeding systems, set up handling and grooming areas, and implement efficient waste management techniques.

The book discusses subjects like understanding mule nutritional needs, developing balanced meals, preventive health care measures, managing common health disorders, and working with vets and farriers for maximum mule health. Nutrition and health care are crucial for mule welfare.

A harmonious and fruitful relationship between farmers and their mules is ensured by the book's advice on developing trust, teaching commands, handling behavioral issues, handling basic training techniques, and advancing training for working mules. Training and handling mules are crucial skills for farm success.

In addition, the book explores future trends and innovations in mule farming, common misconceptions, problem-solving, FAQs, working mules in agricultural operations, disease management, financial planning, marketing strategies for mules and mule products, and connecting with mule farming communities for ongoing support and education.

"Complete Guide to Mule Farming" provides a thorough and all-encompassing coverage of every facet of mule farming. It does so by combining expert insights, interesting information, and practical recommendations to enhance the reader's comprehension and skill level in mule farming operations.

CHAPTER ONE
INTRODUCTION TO MULE FARMING
RECOGNIZING THE FUNCTION OF MULES IN AGRICULTURE

Success in mule farming depends on having a solid understanding of the function of mules. Mules are intelligent, strong, and long-lived hybrids that were created by crossing a female horse with a male donkey. Because of their versatility in doing activities like pulling carts, carrying goods, and plowing fields, they have been utilized in farming for millennia. Because they are tough, steady on their feet, and able to work long hours without becoming tired easily, mules are chosen over horses in many farming operations.

Effectively training and working with mules is a crucial part of mule farming. Although intelligent animals, mules need to be handled gently yet firmly. Training mules is employing regular cues and rewarding reinforcement to teach them directions like stop, go, turn, and back up.

Comprehending their innate tendencies and inclinations, such as their robust self-defense mechanism, facilitates the establishment of a peaceful cooperative partnership with them on the farm.

Mules are also essential to sustainable agricultural methods. Being able to work effectively without depending too much on machines lowers fuel consumption and carbon emissions, which makes them environmentally beneficial agricultural partners. All things considered, an effective and profitable mule farming endeavor begins with an understanding of the importance of mules in farming operations.

ADVANTAGES OF FARMING MULES

Mule farming is a desirable alternative for farmers because of its many and varied benefits. The mule's capacity to adapt to different farm tasks is one of its main assets. Mules are capable of plowing fields, hauling huge loads, hauling equipment, and even being a farmer's trusted labor partner. They are important assets in agricultural operations because of their strength and endurance, particularly in places where access to machinery may be restricted.

The affordability of mule farming in comparison to other animal or machinery-based methods is another important advantage. Because of their lifespan and low maintenance needs, mules help farmers operate more profitably overall. They are an affordable and sustainable option for many farmers since they can survive on basic diets, require less veterinary care, and have longer working lives than some other farm animals.

Mule farming also encourages sustainable agricultural methods. Mules are kinder to the earth than heavy machinery, which helps maintain the fertility and structure of the soil. They are appropriate for a variety of farming situations due to their versatility in handling different types of terrain, such as rough or hilly places. Mule farming has several advantages, including reduced costs, sustainable environmental practices, and dependable farm output.

ESSENTIAL TERMS FOR MULE FARMING

Knowing the fundamental terms used in mule farming is crucial for efficient management and communication. Some essential terms to understand are:

• Mule: A crossbreed between a female horse and a male donkey, prized for its power and adaptability in agricultural work.

• Hinny: A crossbreeds between a male horse and a female donkey; resembles a mule but differs slightly in appearance and behavior.

• Draft Mule: Because of its size, strength, and endurance, a draft mule is bred especially and trained for heavy work, like pulling wagons or plows.

• Pack Mule: A mule that has been trained to haul burdens on its back; these animals are frequently utilized for camping, hiking, and hauling cargo over difficult terrain.

• Harness: A piece of equipment with straps, buckles, and fittings for securing mules to carts, plows, or other work tools.

• Hitch: The process of utilizing a harness to secure mules to a vehicle or other object to ensure their safety and correct alignment while working.

Acquainting oneself with these terminologies and their definitions promotes easy communication and comprehension among the mule farming community. It helps farmers to efficiently discuss work duties, equipment use, training techniques, and other mule-related matters, improving overall operational efficiency and management.

SAFETY MEASURES AND THE WELFARE OF ANIMALS

For the sake of the health and welfare of the mules as well as the farm laborers, safety measures and animal welfare are crucial in mule farming. By putting in place the right safety precautions, everyone's chance of an accident, injury, and stress is decreased. In mule farming, some crucial safety measures are as follows:

• Appropriate Training: To reduce dangers during labor activities, thoroughly instruct farm workers and mules on handling procedures, equipment operation, and safety standards.

• Routine Maintenance: Keep facilities, harnesses, and equipment in good working order to avoid breakdowns or malfunctions that could put mules or employees at risk.

• Watching the Weather: To avoid heat exhaustion, dehydration, or frostbite, work mules should not be exposed to extreme heat or cold.

• Emergency Preparedness: Establish backup plans and protocols to handle mishaps, wounds, or unexpected medical problems affecting staff members or mules.

• Animal Welfare Practices: To support the health, comfort, and productivity of mules on the farm, makes sure they receive the right food, water, rest, and medical attention.

Mule farmers prioritize animal health and safety to establish a safe and secure environment that is favorable to successful farming operations. Mule farming techniques become sustainable and prosperous as a result of the culture of accountability, professionalism, and care it cultivates.

ORGANIZING YOUR MULE FARMING BUSINESS

To get the best results, mule farming operations need to be set up with meticulous planning, preparation, and execution. The following are some crucial actions in starting a mule farm:

• Choosing Appropriate Land: Pick a plot of land that has enough room, rich soil, water supplies nearby, and suitable terrain for mule activities like working, grazing, and exercising.

• Building Facilities: To ensure the safety and functionality of mule housing, feeding, and equipment storage, build or renovate barns, shelters, fences, and storage facilities.

• Purchasing Mules: Buy or breed mules that are appropriate for the specified farming activities, taking into account aspects like training, temperament, size, age, and health history.

• Purchasing Equipment: To ensure efficiency and safety during agricultural operations, spend money on high-quality equipment, tools, and machinery for mule training, handling, grooming, and labor chores.

• Creating Work Plans: To maximize productivity and well-being, create thorough work plans, schedules, and routines for mules. These should include training sessions, food schedules, exercise regimens, and job assignments.

For more assistance, direction, and resources, forming alliances with veterinary specialists, agricultural specialists, and other mule farmers can be quite beneficial.

CHAPTER TWO

CHOOSING AND PURCHASING MULES

SELECTING THE BEST BREEDS OF MULES FOR YOUR FARM

It's important to keep your farm's intended use in mind while choosing mule breeds. For example, robust breeds with power and endurance, such as Belgian mule crosses or Percheron, are great options if your concentration is agricultural work. On the other hand, a smaller, more agile breed like the Tennessee Walking Mule would be more appropriate if your farm needs mules for packing or trail riding. Finding out more about different mule breeds and their traits is essential to making a wise choice.

In addition to the planned use, take your farm's climate and topography into account. Some mule breeds are more suited to particular types of situations. For example, a mule breed like the Rocky Mountain Mule, which is durable and sure-footed, would be perfect if your farm is situated in a mountainous area.

In a similar vein, mules tolerant of hot and muggy weather—like the Florida Cracker Mule—would be useful if you happen to be in one.

Evaluate your knowledge and proficiency with mules as well. Select a breed that corresponds with your level of expertise, as certain varieties could demand more handling and training than others. Speaking with knowledgeable breeders or mule farmers can also provide you with important information about which breeds are ideal for your particular agricultural requirements.

ASSESSING THE AGE AND HEALTH OF MULES

The first step in assessing mule age and health is to look at their general state. Keep a watch out for indicators of good health, like a glossy coat, bright eyes, and attentive demeanor. Look for any anomalies, such as respiratory problems, lameness, or malnourishment symptoms. To make sure the mule is healthy; a comprehensive physical examination must be performed by you or a veterinarian.

Age is yet another important consideration. Compared to older, more seasoned mules, younger mules could need more handling and training. Older mules, however, can have health problems or a limited amount of years left to labor. Achieve a balance between the requirements of your farm and your capacity to train and handle a range of ages of mules.

If the mule has a past employment history, take that into account. Mules in good condition and with a track record of success might be well worth the investment, particularly if they meet the needs of your farm. Mule health must be maintained and their working lives must be extended on your farm through regular health examinations and appropriate care.

BUYING MULES FROM RELIABLE VENDORS

It's essential to get mules from reliable providers for your farm to guarantee that the animals you receive are healthy and well-trained. Investigate respectable farms or breeders of mules who have a track record of producing high-quality mules. Go to mule shows or auctions where respectable breeders display their stock.

Examine the mules carefully before deciding to buy them. Keep an eye out for any indications of behavioral or health concerns. Inquire with the vendor about the mule's background, including its training, employment history, and medical documents. A reliable vendor will be open and honest with you, and they could even let you do a final inspection before completing the deal.

Steer clear of buying mules from unidentified or dubious sources as they can be hiding behavioral or physical problems. Purchasing mules from reliable vendors guarantees the animals' quality and offers continuing support and direction from knowledgeable breeders or merchants.

MULE TRANSPORTATION AND INTRODUCTION TO YOUR FARM

It takes meticulous planning to ensure the safety and comfort of the mules when they are being transported to your property. Make use of a livestock trailer that is appropriate for the purpose, with enough room for the mules to stand comfortably and adequate restraints to keep them from getting hurt. When planning the itinerary, keep in mind that the mules may become stressed by tough terrain or severe weather.

When the mules arrive at your farm, acclimate them gradually to their new surroundings. Give food, water, and shelter to a specific area. Before acclimating the mules to other animals or initiating work-related tasks, give them some time to settle in and become acquainted with their environment.

During the first few days, keep a tight eye on the mules to make sure they are eating, drinking, and acting properly. To achieve a seamless transition, keep an eye out for any indications of tension or pain and adjust as necessary. It is essential to properly acclimate mules to your farm to ensure their performance and general well-being.

EXAMS FOR HEALTH AND QUARANTINE FOR NEW MULES

For the sake of your farm's mule population's general health and to stop the spread of disease, you must implement a quarantine period and do comprehensive health tests on new mules. For incoming mules, set aside a distinct quarantine area that is isolated from other animals.

Keep an eye out for any symptoms of disease in the mules during the quarantine period, such as coughing, nasal discharge, or lethargy. Keep an eye on the temperature, inspect the feces for parasites, and administer immunizations by veterinarian advice as part of routine health checks.

To create a quarantine and health check schedule that is unique to your farm and the requirements of the mules, speak with a veterinarian. Follow biosecurity protocols to stop the spread of disease from isolated mules to other members of your farm's populace.

CHAPTER THREE

MULE HOUSING AND AMENITIES

CREATING APPROPRIATE STABLES AND BARNS

To guarantee your animals' happiness and welfare while designing barns and stables for mule farming, there are several important factors to take into account. The first stage is to determine how many miles you intend to maintain and what kind of space and shelter you require. Each mule should have enough room to walk about comfortably in a well-designed barn, which should have distinct spaces for eating, sleeping, and sheltering from the weather.

Think about things like flooring, lighting, and ventilation while planning the barn's layout. Sufficient ventilation is essential to avoid respiratory problems and preserve the barn's air quality. In addition to saving energy, natural lighting improves the living conditions for caregivers and mules alike.

To protect the animals' health and safety, the flooring needs to be non-slip and simple to maintain.

Include bedding, equipment, and feed storage sections in the barn as well. Maintaining order and cleanliness through proper storage promotes effective farm management. To construct a barn that satisfies the unique requirements of mule farming while upholding safety and legal requirements, think about speaking with knowledgeable farmers or agricultural engineers.

OPTIONS FOR MULE ENCLOSURE FENCING

For the safety and security of your mule enclosures, selecting the appropriate fencing is crucial. Mule farming can benefit from a variety of fencing systems, each with pros and downsides. Although wooden fences are aesthetically pleasing and long-lasting, they need to be regularly maintained to avoid decay and damage. Electric fences work well to keep mules from trying to break free, but they need to be regularly checked for functionality and power.

Cost-effective and offering excellent visibility, mesh wire fences confine mules. Fences made of pipe and cable are durable and strong, which makes them ideal for larger properties that house several mules. Whatever kind of fencing you choose, make sure it is both solid and tall enough to keep mules from jumping over it and from pushing it occasionally.

Maintain and repair fences regularly to avoid potential escape routes and fix any damage. For quick access to various farm areas and effective handling of mules during daily routines and veterinary care, think about erecting gates at key locations.

SYSTEMS FOR WATERING AND FEEDING

Putting in place effective feeding and watering systems is essential for the health and welfare of the mules on your property. When planning irrigation systems, take into account the available water sources—such as ponds, wells, or city water—and make sure that there is always access to fresh, clean water.

Particularly in the summer, automatic waterers can be useful in helping to constantly maintain water levels.

Design feeding areas for feeding systems such that they can hold the number of mules and that hay and feed can be easily accessed. Feeders that reduce waste and contamination, like hay racks or covered feed bins, should be used. Create a feeding program that satisfies the dietary needs of mules according to their age, degree of exercise, and overall health while offering a balanced diet.

Watering and feeding systems should be routinely cleaned and maintained to avoid contamination and guarantee optimal performance. To spot any changes or health problems early on and modify feeding schedules appropriately, keep an eye on the amount of water and feed that the mules are consuming. Veterinary or nutritionist advice might help develop a feeding plan that is specifically tailored to the requirements of your mules.

For mules to be managed well and to retain their health and attractiveness, adequate handling and grooming areas must be created. When designing handling facilities, consider including robust gates and chutes to enable mules to move safely and under control during tasks like immunizations, clipping hooves, and loading onto trailers. To avoid mishaps and guarantee the comfort of mules during handling processes, provide flooring that is not slippery.

Roomy grooming rooms with plenty of horse grooming supplies including combs, brushes, and hoof picks are essential. To secure mules during grooming procedures, think about putting tie-up posts or cross-ties. Establish distinct spaces for handling and grooming to avoid cross-contamination and preserve hygiene.

Establish a program for regular grooming that involves brushing, maintaining the mane and tail, caring for the hooves, and taking baths as needed. In addition to improving equine appearance, proper grooming fosters animal-caregiver attachment. To protect the welfare of mules and reduce stress during these tasks, personnel or volunteers should get training on appropriate handling and grooming techniques.

PUTTING WASTE MANAGEMENT PRACTICES INTO PRACTICE

Keeping your mule farm clean and hygienic requires putting proper waste management techniques into place. Create a plan for the routine removal and disposal of waste, like as manure and soiled bedding, by first identifying the places where it collects. If you want to produce nutrient-rich fertilizer for your farm or to sell to nearby gardeners, think about composting organic waste.

To avoid contamination and odor problems, set aside particular spaces for the storage, composting, and disposal of waste. Keep these spaces far from the mule living and grazing areas. Based on the size and number of mules on the farm, install suitable trash containers (such as compost bins or dumpsters) and create a plan for garbage collection and removal.

Teach volunteers and farm employees safe disposal techniques and appropriate waste management techniques, such as recycling non-organic waste options. Check waste management facilities regularly to make sure they are in compliance with environmental rules and need maintenance. Using effective waste management techniques enhances farm productivity overall and environmental sustainability in addition to improving farm aesthetics.

CHAPTER FOUR

CONSUMPTION AND MEDICAL CARE

RECOGNIZING THE NUTRITIOUS NEEDS OF MULES

Due to their hybrid nature, mules have special dietary needs that are marginally different from those of horses and donkeys. It is essential to comprehend these requirements for their success and well-being. Mules typically need a well-balanced diet that includes grains like oats or barley in addition to premium fodder like alfalfa or grass hay. To prevent overfeeding, which can result in obesity and other health problems, their nutrition should be closely watched.

Mules require specialized nutrition such as enough protein for muscular growth and repair and energy sources such as lipids and carbohydrates for warmth and activity. They also need some vital vitamins and minerals, like electrolytes for nerve function and hydration, calcium for strong bones, and vitamin A for the immune system and vision. It is critical to their well-being to always have access to clean water.

MAKING WELL-BALANCED MEALS FOR MULES

Mules must have a balanced diet, which means determining what nutrients they need and adjusting their feed accordingly. As the base of their diet, start with high-quality fodder that has been cleared of dust and mold. When necessary, add grains and concentrates to this, taking into account your age, degree of exercise, and general health. To prevent upset stomachs, new feeds must be introduced gradually.

To avoid under- or overfeeding, periodically assess their physical condition and modify their food accordingly. To satisfy their mineral requirements, provide them access to salt blocks or mineral supplements. To create a customized feeding plan, especially for mules with particular health issues or performance objectives, speak with an equine nutritionist. Mule longevity, performance, and general health are all enhanced by a well-balanced diet.

HEALTH CARE PREVENTIVE MEASURES

To protect the health and productivity of mule farmers, preventive healthcare is essential. This covers routine immunizations against prevalent equine illnesses like West Nile virus, influenza, and tetanus. To avoid parasite infestations, create a deworming program based on fecal egg counts and rotating deworming techniques. To reduce the chance of contracting infectious diseases, keep the surroundings tidy and secure.

Regular dental care is also necessary since, similar to horses, mules need to have floating and dental exams regularly to avoid dental problems that could influence their eating patterns and general health. Another essential component of preventive healthcare is hoof care, which includes routine shoeing and trimming by a licensed farrier to preserve healthy hoof balance and function. The health and lifespan of the mules on the farm are guaranteed by proactively putting these preventive measures into practice.

COMMON HEALTH PROBLEMS AND SOLUTIONS FOR MULES

Even with precautions, mules may still have health problems that need to be treated right away. Lameness, respiratory infections, skin conditions, and digestive troubles are common health issues. Lameness can be caused by several things, including poor hoof care, injuries, or joint problems. A veterinarian should be consulted for an assessment and treatment, which may involve corrective shoeing, medication, or rest.

Environmental factors such as dust and pollen exposure and inadequate ventilation can lead to respiratory illnesses. As part of treatment, supportive care is given, the underlying cause is addressed, and occasionally antibiotics or anti-inflammatory drugs are given. To prevent recurrence, topical therapies and environmental control may be necessary for skin illnesses such as dermatitis or fungal infections.

Serious digestive issues that call for prompt veterinarian care include colic and stomach ulcers.

Medication, stress management approaches, and dietary modifications are examples of management strategies. Mules may be efficiently managed and treated for common health conditions, assuring their well-being and performance on the farm, with regular monitoring for signs of trouble and early veterinarian intervention.

COLLABORATING WITH FARRIERS AND VETERINARIANS

Working together with farriers and veterinarians is crucial to mule health and well-being. Plan on receiving immunizations, health screenings, and preventive treatment at regular veterinary checkups. To address any difficulties early, discuss with your veterinarian any concerns you may have or any changes in behavior or condition. Develop a cooperative relationship with a knowledgeable farrier for regular hoof care and, if required, corrective shoeing.

When collaborating with veterinary and farrier specialists, communication is essential.

Give them thorough details about your mules' diet, exercise regimen, and any past medical conditions. Pay close attention to their advice regarding treatment regimens, follow-up appointments, and preventive care. Learn the fundamentals of emergency response and first aid so that you can handle medical situations until help arrives.

You may guarantee thorough care for your mules and improve their health, well-being, and performance in farming tasks by actively working with veterinary and farrier specialists.

CHAPTER FIVE

MULE HANDLING AND TRAINING

DEVELOPING RELATIONSHIPS AND TRUST WITH MULES

Establishing rapport and trust with mules is essential to mule farming success. Start by spending daily time with your mules, caressing and combing them gently so they become accustomed to your presence and touch. Since mules are sensitive to human emotions and respond strongly to good interactions, adopt a calm and patient manner when building trust.

Handling your mules regularly with tasks like haltering, tying, and leading them helps them get used to your direction and feel secure. Maintaining a schedule for training, grooming, and feeding will help create a dependable atmosphere that soothes mules. Consistency is essential. Treats can also strengthen trust and establish pleasant associations between you and your mules during training sessions.

Establishing a secure and cozy home atmosphere strengthens bonds and trust even more. Give people plenty of room to move around, access to wholesome food and fresh water, and protection from inclement weather. The relationship between you and your animals is strengthened and mule health and general well-being are enhanced by routine veterinarian care.

FUNDAMENTAL TRAINING METHODS FOR MULE HANDLING

The basis for proficient mule handling is laid by using fundamental training methods. Introduce fundamental commands like "walk," "halt," and "back up" first, being sure to use consistent motions and unambiguous vocal cues. Reward desired conduct in mules by giving them praise, scratches, or goodies to motivate them to obey directions on time.

Lunging and leading are examples of groundwork exercises that assist mules in understanding boundaries and gaining respect for their authority. Regular practice of these exercises can help you and your mules become more coordinated and communicate better. To prevent discomfort or resistance, gradually expose them to wearing a saddle and bridle, making sure that it fits and feels comfortable.

Mules are easier to train when they have a routine in place for grooming, hoof care, and handling feet because it keeps them relaxed and cooperative. It's important to be persistent and patient; pushing or hurrying mules to do things they're not ready for might cause frustration and resistance.

INSTRUCTING IN SIGNALS AND COMMANDS

Mule training must include teaching signs and commands for them to communicate effectively. Beginning with simple orders such as "whoa," "walk on," "turn," and "back up," employ consistent indications in speech and matching body language. These commands should be reinforced with repetition and positive rewards until mules consistently obey your signals.

It's important to be consistent; employ the same cues and signals regularly to prevent misunderstandings and develop a good rapport with your mules. Once mules are comfortable with the fundamentals—such as lateral movements, transitions between gaits, and navigating obstacles—you can gradually add more complex commands and signals.

During training sessions, reinforce commands and signals with training aids like flags, whips, or clickers. To guarantee effective communication and comprehension, use patience, pay attention to mule replies, and modify your strategy as necessary. Over time, regular exercise and reinforcement of directions aid in the retention of training and increase the responsiveness of mules.

MANAGING DIFFICULTIES AND BEHAVIORAL PROBLEMS

Mule farming entails dealing with difficulties and behavioral problems. Common problems include intransigence, fear-based responses, and resistance to handling. To overcome behavioral roadblocks, approach these problems with tolerance, understanding, and regular training methods.

To create focused remedies, determine the underlying causes of behavioral problems, such as uncomfortable situations in the past or a lack of trust. To assist mules in progressively overcoming fear or resistance, break things down into smaller, more doable steps. To promote desirable actions and boost confidence, use prizes and positive reinforcement.

If you are dealing with persistent or complicated behavioral problems, get expert advice or speak with knowledgeable mule trainers. Work together with specialists to create specialized training programs and approaches that are suited to certain problems. Many behavioral problems may be fixed with persistence, patience, and a proactive attitude, which will enhance overall mule management and farm output.

ADVANCED INSTRUCTION FOR OPERATIONAL MULES

Working mules must receive advanced training to be prepared for particular duties and obligations on the farm. Improve your ability to respond, hone your directions and signals, and introduce specific abilities that are necessary for farm work, such as hauling carts, plowing fields, or lifting goods.

When mules get more confident and skilled in their foundational training, gradually increase the complexity of tasks and demands. Training sessions should incorporate real-world events and difficulties to imitate farm work environments and get mules ready to apply their abilities in real-world situations.

To improve mule versatility and talents, use advanced training tools and methods such as obstacle courses, harnesses, and implements. Closely monitor the progress of the mule, correcting any deviations and reinforcing desired behaviors with positive rewards and feedback.

CHAPTER SIX

BREEDING AND REPRODUCTION OF MULES

KNOWING THE BIOLOGY OF MULE REPRODUCTION

Understanding the biology of mule reproduction is essential to effective breeding programs and understanding how mules reproduce, making it an intriguing facet of mule farming. Mules are crossbred animals that are produced when a female horse (mare) and a male donkey (jack) mate. Understanding this hybridization process is crucial because it affects the developing mules' genetic makeup, disposition, and physical attributes.

Knowing the female mule's estrous cycle is essential to mule reproduction. The reproductive cycles of female mules, sometimes referred to as molly mules, are distinct and impacted by the reproductive cycles of both donkeys and horses. Since they usually enter estrus, or heat, at specified seasons, timing is essential to effective reproduction. Furthermore, an understanding of the anatomy and physiology of mules about reproduction—including the composition of the reproductive organs and the effects of hormones—helps in the efficient management of breeding programs.

Furthermore, breeders need to understand mule genetics and inheritance patterns. It is easier to choose breeding stock and forecast the features of upcoming mule generations when one is aware of how genetic qualities are handed down from the jack and mare to the mule progeny. Overall, the basis for effective mule farming and breeding activities is a thorough grasp of the biology of mule reproduction.

CHOOSING BREEDING STOCK

To produce healthy and appealing offspring, choosing the proper breeding stock is an essential stage in mule farming. Many considerations, like conformation, temperament, health, and genetic heritage, are taken into account while selecting breeding stock. The term "conformation" describes a mule's general balance, leg conformation, and body shape, among other physical characteristics. Choosing mules with superior conformation helps to produce offspring with desired physical characteristics.

Another important factor to take into account while choosing breeding stock is temperament. It is best to breed mules with calm, trainable temperaments because these qualities are frequently inherited by their progeny. It is imperative to assess the health of prospective breeding stock to guard against genetic health problems and guarantee the welfare of the mules and their progeny.

When choosing breeding stock, genetic background is important since it affects the traits and qualities that are handed down to the next generation. Mules with good genetic lines, coveted attributes, and track records of performance are highly sought after by breeders. Mule farmers can improve the caliber and reliability of their mule breeding operations by carefully choosing breeding stock based on conformation, temperament, health, and genetic heritage.

BREEDING STRATEGIES AND SCHEDULE

For mule farming and reproduction to be successful, it is essential to comprehend breeding techniques and timing. Mule farming employs a variety of breeding techniques, such as embryo transfer, artificial insemination (AI), and natural breeding. In artificial insemination (AI), a mare is artificially inseminated after a jack's semen is extracted, as opposed to natural breeding, which lets a jack and mare mate naturally. A more sophisticated method is called embryo transfer, which is the process of moving embryos from a donor mare to a recipient mare.

One of the most important factors in mule reproduction is when to breed. Estrus, or heat, is a season-specific hormonal and photoperiodic state experienced by female mules. The best time to breed mules is determined by carefully observing the estrous cycles of the females. Coordinating reproductive endeavors with the mare's estrous cycle enhances the likelihood of fruitful mating and pregnancy.

Furthermore, knowing the behavioral and physical cues that indicate a female mule is in estrus aids in determining when it is most conducive to breeding. Mule farmers can increase breeding success rates and produce healthy mule offspring by using appropriate breeding techniques and scheduling mating efforts effectively.

MULE PREGNANCY TREATMENT

The health and welfare of pregnant mules and their unborn foals depend on providing them with the proper care during their pregnancy. After a mule has been successfully mated, it is essential to give her enough food, veterinary attention, and supervision during her pregnancy. For the mule's health to be supported during pregnancy, nutrition is essential. A well-balanced diet full of vital elements, such as protein, vitamins, minerals, and energy sources, is necessary for pregnant mules.

To keep an eye on the mule's health and take quick action in the event of a problem, regular veterinary treatment is crucial throughout pregnancy. Veterinarians can give immunizations, do ultrasounds to monitor the pregnancy's progress, and offer advice on prenatal care. It is easier to guarantee a smooth pregnancy and delivery if the mule's weight, physical condition, and general health are monitored.

For pregnant mules, setting up an appropriate foaling habitat is also essential. Reducing stress and minimizing hazards during labor and birth is achieved by providing a clean, calm, and safe foaling facility. Furthermore, the best potential outcome for the mule and the foal is ensured when a plan is in place for assistance with foaling in case it becomes necessary, such as having a veterinarian on call. Mule farmers may maintain healthy pregnancies and create robust, resilient foals by placing a high priority on prenatal care.

HANDLING AND TAKING CARE OF FOALS

To ensure the healthy development and well-being of newborn mule foals, handling, and care of the foals is an essential part of mule farming. Building trust and fostering pleasant interactions between humans and foals can be achieved by proper handling of the animals from birth. To create a safe and secure atmosphere, it is crucial to handle newborn foals with kindness, patience, and consistency.

One of the most important things a mare can do for her young foals is to make sure they get colostrum, which is her first milk and contains important nutrients and antibodies. For foals, colostrum enhances the development of their immune systems and offers passive immunity. It is helpful to keep an eye on the foal's temperature, heart rate, and nursing habits to spot any possible problems early on.

As foals mature, training, socializing, and a healthy diet become crucial components of their care. Healthy development is facilitated by offering a balanced diet appropriate for developing mules, frequent veterinarian examinations, and chances for socialization with humans and other mules.

Foals that receive basic handling, leading, and manners training will be more equipped for future farm responsibilities and interactions.

In general, raising healthy, well-adjusted mule foals who are prepared to contribute to the mule farming operation requires careful handling and care from birth through the early stages of development.

CHAPTER SEVEN

USING MULES IN AGRICULTURE

MULES' FUNCTIONS IN AGRICULTURE

Mules combine the muscles of horses and the intelligence of donkeys, making them valuable in a variety of farming chores. One of their main responsibilities is draft work, which involves helping to plow fields, towing big objects like produce-filled carts or wagons, and moving equipment throughout the farm. They are perfect for jobs that call for steady, dependable power over long periods because of their strength and endurance.

Mules are also excellent at transportation jobs; they can be used for carrying supplies to various parts of the farm or transporting harvested crops from the fields to storage places. Their agility and skill in navigating difficult terrain make them invaluable, particularly on farms with varied terrain or difficult topography. In addition, mules are frequently employed in livestock herding because of their ability to guide and control sheep or cattle due to their placid nature and innate herding skills.

PREPARING MULES FOR PARTICULAR TASKS

It takes persistence, patience, and an awareness of mules' distinct behavior to train them for particular jobs. Basic obedience training is crucial, and you should give them directions like "walk," "stop," "turn," and "back up." Treats or praise are examples of positive reinforcement strategies that can help reinforce desired actions and build a trusting relationship between the handler and the mule.

It is essential to progressively acclimate mules to harnesses and equipment before assigning them to specific activities like plowing or pulling hefty loads. To develop their strength and confidence, start with small loads and brief sessions before moving on to more difficult assignments. Mules will efficiently learn their roles if they receive consistent training sessions with clear information and mild corrections for undesired conduct.

MULE EQUIPMENT AND HARNESSING

Mules must be properly harnessed and equipped to guarantee their comfort and safety while working on farms. An appropriately fitted harness minimizes friction and irritation while distributing weight uniformly. Correct harness adjustment is essential to prevent any limitations on movement while retaining stability and control, particularly while towing large objects.

Plows, carts, and wagons should all be made of solid materials and the right size for use with mules. To inspect for wear and tear, loose parts, or any indications of damage that could jeopardize safety, equipment must undergo routine maintenance. Before beginning real farm work, mules should be trained to grow accustomed to harnesses and other equipment. This will aid in their acclimatization and increase their productivity.

PRECAUTIONARY STEPS FOR FARM WORK SAFETY

It is crucial to have safety precautions in place when working on farms to shield handlers and mules from potential mishaps or injuries. This includes keeping an orderly and clean work area to avoid impediments or tripping risks, doing routine safety inspections on equipment, and making sure that mules are appropriately trained and prepared for the job at hand.

To reduce the chance of accidents, handlers should always wear the proper safety equipment, such as strong boots, gloves, and helmets when needed. To guide mules and coordinate movements during chores like plowing or harvesting, team members must effectively communicate with one another and use clear signals or directions. Frequent training sessions on emergency protocols and safety measures can also help to reduce risks and provide a secure working environment for all parties.

OPTIMIZING PRODUCTIVITY WITH MULE TEAMS

With mule teams, strategic planning and coordination are essential to maximizing efficiency. Efficient work and less stress can be achieved by allocating responsibilities and duties according to each mule's unique skills and strengths. When mules with complementary skills are paired for duties like plowing or dragging loads, for instance, productivity can be increased and superior outcomes can be obtained.

Mules are prepared and energetic for farm work when training, feeding, and resting schedules are adhered to consistently. To keep mules in top shape and avoid weariness or other health problems that could affect their performance, regular health examinations and appropriate nourishment are also crucial. Mules are further encouraged to work harmoniously as a team when a favorable work environment is provided, which includes clear communication, mutual respect, and awards for outstanding performance. This increases overall farm efficiency.

CHAPTER EIGHT

MULE WELL-BEING AND ILLNESS CONTROL

PRACTICES FOR PREVENTIVE HEALTH

A strong base of preventive healthcare measures is the first step in guaranteeing the health and well-being of your mules. Vaccinations against common infections such as influenza, West Nile virus, and tetanus are essential for prevention. To develop a vaccination program that is customized to your mule's requirements and the risks of local diseases, speak with a veterinarian. To reduce the danger of diseases, make sure the mule barn or pasture is kept clean and sanitary. This entails routinely cleaning the water troughs, getting rid of the dung, and having enough ventilation to prevent respiratory problems.

Another important component of preventive health is proper eating. Make sure your mules always have access to clean water and offer them food that is balanced according to their age, degree of exercise, and overall health. As untreated dental abnormalities might result in digestive concerns, mule health also depends on routine dental checkups. To control internal parasites, follow your veterinarian's suggested deworming regimen. To avoid problems like laminitis, plan routine foot care.

Exercise regularly is also crucial for mule health. To stop obesity and behavioral issues, give people the opportunity for regular exercise and mental stimulation. Regularly check your mule's weight and body condition score so you may make any necessary dietary and exercise adjustments. You can contribute to ensuring your mules live happy and healthy lives by putting these preventive health habits into effect.

IDENTIFYING SYMPTOMS OF DISEASE OR INJURY

Being able to identify symptoms of disease or damage in your mules is essential for timely intervention and care. Changes in appetite, lethargy, unusual behavior, such as pawing or lying down excessively, nasal discharge, coughing, and lameness are typical indicators of disease. To identify any anomalies early on, keep a close eye on your mules' temperature, pulse, and respiration rate.

It's crucial to visually inspect your mules regularly to look for any sores, swellings, or irregularities in their coats or skin. Observe their mannerisms and how they interact with other mules; shifts in social behavior may point to underlying medical problems. When you visit your veterinarian for routine checkups or when you need medical guidance, keep a journal of your mules' health observations and share it with them.

In the event of an accident, administer first aid right away by sterilizing and bandaging injuries, using cold packs to minimize swelling, and, if required, immobilizing limbs. Keep a tight eye out for any indications of shock or distress on the hurt mule, and get veterinary help as soon as possible for additional assessment and care. You can guarantee prompt and efficient care for your mules by being watchful and proactive in identifying symptoms of disease or injury.

In an emergency, knowing the fundamentals of first aid for mules can save lives. First, assemble a first aid package tailored to mule care, with supplies like bandages, wound cleaners, antiseptic ointments, hoof picks, and your veterinarian's emergency contact information. Learn how to perform basic first aid procedures like cleaning and bandaging wounds and taking vital signs.

Cuts and scrapes are examples of small injuries that should be cleaned up with gentle soap and water, treated with antiseptic ointment, and covered with a fresh bandage. Keep an eye out for any indications of infection or worsening of the wound on the mule. In the event of a more severe injury, such as a fracture or deep cuts, stabilize the mule and contact a veterinarian right away.

To give your animals the finest treatment possible in an emergency, you must maintain your composure and concentration. With your family or team, role-play first aid scenarios to make sure everyone understands their roles and responsibilities. To be ready for unforeseen circumstances, periodically check and replenish your emergency response plan and first aid equipment. You can efficiently handle first aid problems for your mules if you are proactive and well-prepared.

IMMUNIZATION AND DISEASE PREVENTION

Vaccination and disease prevention are essential components in managing mule health. Together with your veterinarian, create a vaccination regimen for your mules that takes into account their age, way of life, and risk of disease in the area. For mules, immunizations against rabies, influenza, tetanus, West Nile virus, and equine encephalitis are frequently administered. Make certain that immunizations are given by advised protocols by a registered healthcare provider.

Employ biosecurity measures in addition to immunizations to stop the spread of infectious diseases. This entails establishing quarantine procedures for newly arrived mules at your business, routinely cleaning common areas and equipment, and reducing interactions with mules from other sources. When engaging with mules, wash your hands and wear clean clothes and shoes as a matter of hygiene.

Keep an eye out for any indications of disease in your mules, and notify your veterinarian right once if you notice anything strange. Prompt identification and management of illnesses can greatly enhance results and stop epidemics in your herd of mules. Keep up with local illness trends and make necessary updates to your disease prevention plans. You may contribute to preserving the health and welfare of your mules by making immunization and disease prevention a priority.

PLANNING FOR EMERGENCY REACTIONS

Creating an emergency action plan is essential to managing unforeseen circumstances and reducing hazards to the health and safety of mules. Start by evaluating the risks and dangers that could arise on your mule farm, including accidents, medical issues, and natural disasters.

Make a list of emergency contacts, such as emergency services, your veterinarian, and the local animal control agency.

Make a thorough plan that outlines steps to take in case of an emergency. Include information on emergency shelter locations, evacuation routes, communication methods, and staff or family member roles and duties. To make sure everyone is prepared for emergencies and knows how to act fast, hold frequent training sessions and drills.

Keep a fully packed emergency kit with necessities like water, food, medicine, first aid supplies, and critical paperwork like contact details and medical records. Ensure all staff members are aware of emergency protocols and maintain emergency phone numbers prominently displayed.

Review and update your emergency response plan regularly in light of the lessons you've learned from exercises and real-world incidents. Work together with other farmers or local resources to provide support and assistance to one another in times of need. You can better safeguard your animals and react to unforeseen circumstances if you have a thorough emergency response strategy in place.

CHAPTER NINE

PLANNING AND MANAGEMENT OF FINANCES

SETTING A BUDGET FOR MULE FARMING ACTIVITIES

The first step in creating an efficient budget for mule farming operations is to list all of the required costs. These may cover the price of purchasing mules, feeding, vet care, equipment upkeep, labor, and advertising. You can get a reasonable approximation by looking upmarket pricing in your area and speaking with knowledgeable farmers. Sort these costs into categories of stable (insurance, mortgage payments, etc.) and variable (feed, seasonal labor, etc.). Organizing these numbers and monitoring them over time might be facilitated by making a budget spreadsheet or by using specialized software.

Precisely estimating your income is critical when you have a firm grasp of your expenses. This includes estimating the profits from breeding services, mule sales, and any other associated revenue sources.

When developing these estimates, take into account variables including seasonal swings, competition, and market demand. To control expectations and prevent overestimating profits, a cautious approach to income estimation can be helpful.

Finally, make frequent reviews and adjustments to your budget in light of your actual spending and income. Take note of any differences or areas that require improvement by comparing your budgeted statistics with the actual results. Better financial management and decision-making are made possible by this iterative process on the farm, guaranteeing that resources are distributed effectively to support sustainable operations.

SOURCES OF INCOME FOR MULE FARMING

Selling mules is not the only source of income from mule farming. Mule sales are a major source of income since healthy, well-trained mules can command high prices in the marketplace. Breeding services also make a big difference, particularly if you have good breeding stock and a solid business reputation.

Moreover, providing boarding or training for mules might create consistent revenue sources.

In mule farming, financial stability is largely dependent on diversifying sources of income. For mule lovers or novices, think about providing informative courses or excursions on mule care and training. These endeavors not only bring in money but also strengthen community ties and advertise your farm. You may also increase your revenue by selling mule-related items like equipment, gear, and even branded clothing.

A regular evaluation of consumer preferences and market changes can aid in the discovery of new revenue prospects. For example, you can take advantage of rising trends to diversify your revenue streams, such as the need for leisure riding experiences or mule treatment programs. You may maximize your earning potential while meeting the needs of your target market by continuing to be innovative and flexible.

MAINTAINING DOCUMENTS AND ANALYZING FINANCES

Maintaining accurate records is crucial to handling the financial aspects of mule farming. To begin, arrange financial records in a methodical fashion, including bank statements, tax records, invoices, and receipts. To keep correct records and guarantee adherence to financial requirements, think about utilizing accounting software or employing a professional accountant.

Better financial analysis is possible when revenue and expenses are tracked regularly. To evaluate the farm's financial situation, use instruments such as cash flow estimates, balance sheets, and profit and loss statements. Determine the profitable regions as well as the places where expenses can be cut or optimized. Observing trends over time can also shed light on how revenue streams are affected by market forces or seasonal fluctuations.

Maintain detailed records on mule health, breeding, and performance information in addition to financial records. Making educated management decisions is made easier with the use of this information, which also increases the value of mules sold or breeding services provided. Keeping thorough records and performing frequent financial assessments will help you make better decisions and increase the farm's long-term profitability.

RISK MANAGEMENT AND INSURANCE

Insurance is essential for reducing the risks connected to mule farming activities. Assess possible hazards first, such as crop loss, theft, liability from accidents, and property damage. Find out which insurance policies are best for your farm's requirements by speaking with insurance companies that specialize in agricultural coverage.

Property insurance is a common insurance plan for mule farms, protecting buildings, machinery, and cattle. Liability insurance is also necessary because it pays for both legal costs and injuries to guests or clients. Take into account supplemental insurance for specific risks such as horse death or unplanned company disruption.

Using risk management techniques in addition to insurance increases agricultural protection. This can involve putting in place biosecurity measures to stop disease outbreaks, keeping safe premises and fences to prevent accidents, and having emergency plans ready for natural disasters. To ensure complete protection for your mule farm and to adjust to changing conditions, examine and update insurance plans and risk management procedures regularly.

STRATEGIES FOR LONG-TERM SUSTAINABILITY

Mule farming must strike a balance between social responsibility, environmental preservation, and economic viability to be long-term sustainable. Begin by evaluating how your farming practices—such as water use, trash disposal, and land conservation—affect the environment.

To reduce your ecological footprint, use sustainable farming practices such as composting, rotational grazing, and the use of renewable energy sources.

Enhancing sustainability can also be accomplished by upgrading farm equipment and infrastructure. Installing energy-efficient irrigation and lighting systems, for instance, gradually lowers operational expenses and resource use.

By using precision farming technologies, productivity and efficiency are increased and input usage is reduced when mule health, nutrition, and pasture management are monitored.

To promote social sustainability, interact with stakeholders and your local community. Engage in outreach educational activities, lend support to neighborhood projects, and place a high value on the humane treatment of agricultural laborers and mules. Having a good rapport with neighbors, suppliers, and consumers builds a network of support for long-term success and good effects.

Always assess and modify your sustainability plans in light of new developments in the field, industry best practices, and stakeholder input.

You can guarantee resilient and sustainable growth for your mule farming endeavor by incorporating social, environmental, and economic factors into your farm management strategy.

CHAPTER TEN

PROMOTING PRODUCTS AND MULES

PUTTING YOUR MULE FARM'S BRANDING TO USE

Establishing a strong brand is crucial to differentiating your mule farm from competitors. Establish your farm's unique selling proposition (USP), or what makes it stand out from the competition, first. This might be your use of high-quality mule breeds, sustainable agricultural methods, or specialty mule goods. Create an engaging brand narrative that speaks to your target market and conveys your love of mule farming and the principles your farm upholds.

Next, develop a distinctive visual identity that includes a logo, color palette, and branding components that are used consistently throughout all media. This builds consumer trust and aids in brand awareness. To promote your brand, use social networking sites, a well-designed website, and conventional marketing supplies like business cards and brochures.

To develop a devoted following, interact with your audience through educational content, behind-the-scenes looks at farm life, and client endorsements.

Maintain a close eye on your brand's performance, ask for consumer input, and make the required corrections to stay competitive. In addition to drawing clients, a powerful brand creates chances for alliances, sponsorships, and teamwork, all of which raise the profile and standing of your farm.

STRATEGIES FOR PROMOTION AND ADVERTISING

To reach your target market and create interest in your mule farm and products, you must implement effective advertising and promotion techniques. Start by determining who your target market is and getting to know their needs, preferences, and buying habits. This will help you develop customized advertising efforts that appeal to prospective clients. To reach a varied audience, use a combination of offline and online media, including agricultural trade exhibitions, local newspapers, social media advertisements, and Google Ads.

Make engaging content that emphasizes the advantages of your farm's methods, products, and mule breeds. Share client endorsements, show off your mules in action, and highlight the various uses for your mule goods with stunning photos and films. Utilize influencer alliances, joint ventures with other companies, and marketing campaigns like farm visits and seminars to generate talk and interest.

Using analytics tools, measure important indicators like website traffic, social media interaction, and sales conversions to evaluate the success of your advertising initiatives.

Based on performance statistics, modify your strategy and concentrate on the channels and messaging that most appeal to your target demographic. Efforts to advertise your mule farm business should be deliberate and consistent to increase customer acquisition, brand recognition, and overall business growth.

PROVIDING PRODUCTS AND MULES FOR SALE

It takes a calculated approach to selling mules and mule items to draw clients, present your products, and ensure smooth transactions. Create a website or online storefront first so that buyers may peruse your mules for sale, check out product details, and make purchases. Make sure your website is optimized for search engines, responsive to mobile devices, and easy to navigate for better visibility and natural search traffic.

Employ expert photographs and thorough explanations to highlight the special attributes and characteristics of every item or product. To foster trust and simplify the purchasing process, provide a range of payment choices, safe checkout procedures, and clear pricing. Use customer ratings and reviews to offer social evidence and assist prospective customers in making wise judgments.

Use social media promos, email newsletters, and targeted marketing efforts to advertise your mules and merchandise.

To generate urgency and promote purchases, draw attention to exclusive offers, discounts, or time-limited promotions. Increase average order value and customer satisfaction by using customer data and insights to personalize suggestions and upsell related products.

Throughout the sales process, deliver great customer service by providing warranties, return policies, and post-purchase assistance to foster enduring relationships with your clients. To respond to shifting consumer tastes and market demands, track sales success, evaluate client feedback, and modify your sales tactics. A successful mule farm depends on repeat business generated by consistent sales efforts and first-rate customer service.

RELATIONSHIP MANAGEMENT WITH CUSTOMERS

Developing a close relationship with your clients, increasing their loyalty, and encouraging repeat business all depend on effective customer relationship management (CRM). To begin, divide up your clientele into groups according to their inclinations, past purchases, and levels of interaction. This enables you to target certain client segments with offers and content that are relevant to them, personalizing your marketing and communication efforts.

Track customer interactions, handle questions and feedback, and automate communication procedures with CRM software or tools. Send out newsletters, individualized messages, and email marketing campaigns to remain in touch with customers, share farm updates, and advertise new goods and services. To keep involved and connected, encourage customers to sign up for newsletters, follow you on social media, or join loyalty programs.

Provide outstanding customer service by attending to concerns, answering questions, and finding efficient solutions to problems. Utilize evaluations and comments to enhance your offerings in terms of goods and services as well as the general clientele. Establish a customer feedback loop and use focus groups, surveys, and polls to get feedback to make data-driven decisions.

Create enduring connections with your clients by involving them in community projects, farm events, and instructional materials. Express gratitude with individualized notes of thanks, special discounts, or loyalty and advocacy programs. You may develop brand champions who actively market your mule farm and products to others by putting a high priority on customer connections and providing value that goes beyond sales. This will lead to sustained development and success.

INCREASING MARKET CAPABILITY

Reaching new clients and increasing your mule farm business need to broaden your market reach. To begin with, carry out market research to find emerging markets, trends, and areas for prospective growth in the mule farming sector. Analyze the demands of your customers, your rivals, and any gaps or niches that your farm can cover.

Expand the range of products you offer to cater to various client or market sectors.

To reach a wider audience, think of branching out into other industries like mule training services, equine therapy courses, or eco-tourism excursions. Work together with like-minded companies, associations, or influencers to penetrate new markets and take advantage of their current clientele and networks.

To boost online presence and draw in organic traffic, spend money on digital strategies for marketing that include social media advertising, content marketing, and search engine optimization (SEO).

Provide informative content, like as blog entries, videos, or tutorials, that highlight your mule farming experience, solve problems for customers, and addresses their concerns.

To increase your distribution channels and attract customers outside of your local area, look into collaboration opportunities with distributors, retailers, or online marketplaces.

CHAPTER ELEVEN

UPCOMING DEVELOPMENTS AND TRENDS IN MULE FARMING

NEW DEVELOPMENTS IN MULE FARMING TECHNOLOGIES

When it comes to mule farming, modern farmers looking for productivity and efficiency must embrace emerging technologies. Precision agriculture is one example of this kind of technology; it makes use of drones and GPS systems to monitor and control crop health and irrigation, maximizing output while preserving resources. The integration of intelligent sensors and automated feeding systems in barns guarantees that mules receive the best possible care and nutrition, improving their overall health and productivity.

Furthermore, improvements in genetic engineering have made it possible for breeders to create mules with desired characteristics including resistance to disease, high rates of reproduction, and greater strength.

In addition to increasing output, these genetically modified mules also lessen the need for veterinary care, supporting environmentally friendly agricultural methods.

In addition, mule farmers may now address consumer aspirations for ethical and ecologically friendly products by tracing the origins of their products, certifying organic techniques, and facilitating transparent supply networks through the use of blockchain technology. Mule farmers will be able to precisely and strategically negotiate the intricacies of contemporary agriculture by utilizing these cutting-edge technologies.

ENVIRONMENTAL IMPACT AND SUSTAINABLE PRACTICES

Mule farmers are adopting more sustainable techniques as stewards of the land to reduce their negative effects on the environment and maintain their long-term profitability. By putting rotational grazing systems into place, land may be used more effectively while also improving soil health and biodiversity.

By increasing soil fertility and decreasing dependency on synthetic chemicals, cover crops and organic fertilizers help reduce nutrient runoff into water sources.

Additionally, using integrated pest management techniques keeps beneficial insect populations intact and preserves ecological equilibrium by lowering the demand for pesticides. Long-term operational expenses are also decreased by investing in renewable energy sources like wind turbines and solar panels, which help lessen carbon footprint.

Additionally, conserving water by using rainwater collection systems and drip irrigation systems not only protects this valuable resource but also increases crop resistance to drought.

Mule farmers can protect ecosystems, satisfy consumer demand for environmentally friendly goods, and create resilient agricultural systems for the future by making sustainability a top priority in their operations.

INITIATIVES FOR EDUCATION AND TRAINING

Mule farming techniques are being advanced by education and training, which also equips farmers with newfound information and abilities. Workshops, seminars, and online courses on subjects including breeding methods, company development tactics, and mule health management are examples of educational endeavors.

Training programs ensure that safety procedures are followed and best practices are maintained by providing practical experience in mule handling, harnessing, and equipment operation. Working with research centers and agricultural colleges gives access to cutting-edge discoveries and research, encouraging lifelong learning and adaptability.

Additionally, mentorship programs match up novice and seasoned farmers to transmit expertise and create a network of like-minded mule aficionados. Mule farmers may improve their knowledge, streamline farm operations, and support a vibrant agriculture industry by investing in education and training.

INTERNATIONAL MARKET PROSPECTS

Mule farmers have a lot of great options to reach a wider audience and take advantage of a variety of customer trends and tastes thanks to the worldwide market. There are opportunities for revenue growth and market diversification when mule goods like meat, wool, and leather are exported to other markets.

Furthermore, farmers can promote their products to a worldwide audience, increase brand recognition, and promote direct-to-consumer sales by utilizing e-commerce platforms and digital marketing techniques. Farmers can network with industry players, look into joint ventures, and remain up to date on market trends by taking part in trade shows, expos, and agricultural events.

Additionally, making changes to items to comply with international certifications and standards guarantees regulatory compliance and boosts market competitiveness. Mule farmers may establish themselves as major players in the agricultural export market and support regional economic growth by seizing chances in the global market.

ADJUSTMENT TO SHIFTING MARKET CONDITIONS

Mule farmers need to be flexible and sensitive to shifting industry dynamics to survive in a fast-changing agricultural landscape. By keeping an eye on customer preferences and market trends, farmers may predict changes in demand and modify production to maximize profitability and resource allocation.

Furthermore, increasing the variety of products offered and providing value-added services like farm-to-table programs, educational workshops, and agritourism experiences boosts client loyalty and engagement. Using digital technologies to automate marketing, analyze data, and manage farms simplifies operations and enhances decision-making.

Furthermore, farmers may stay ahead of the curve and take advantage of new opportunities by keeping up to date on industry developments, technical advancements, and legislative changes through networking forums and industry groups. Mule farmers may negotiate obstacles, take advantage of opportunities, and create sustainable agricultural operations for the future by adjusting to changing industry conditions.

CHAPTER TWELVE

COMMON QUESTIONS AND EXTENSIVE ANSWERS

DISPELLING FREQUENTLY HELD MYTHS ABOUT MULE FARMING

There are several myths surrounding mule farming that can discourage newcomers. The idea that mules are obstinate and challenging to work with is a frequent one. In actuality, mules are bright, flexible animals that respond well to training when given the right tools and patience. There is also a misperception that mules are not as strong or as effective as horses. Although mules may not be as proficient as horses in every aspect, they do have certain advantages like endurance and sure footing that make them useful for specific jobs.

Another myth is that mules are only meant for work and are incapable of developing strong emotional attachments or affection. There is no way that this is not the case. When given kindness and respect, mules can form close relationships with their handlers and exhibit affection and responsiveness. In addition, some could believe that, in contrast to other livestock endeavors, mule farming is neither sustainable nor profitable. But for those who value the distinctive attributes mules offer, mule farming can be a profitable and fulfilling endeavor with the right management.

SOLVING TYPICAL PROBLEMS FOR NOVICES

Mule farming novices frequently run into typical problems that can be avoided with planning and understanding. Understanding mule behavior and communication is one prevalent problem. Mules have a unique way of expressing themselves, and newcomers may mistake their behavior for disobedience or stubbornness. Gaining a grasp of mule body language and cues can aid enhance handling methods and avoid miscommunications.

Taking care of the health and diet of mules is another frequent problem. Novices could have trouble choosing the proper diet and medical regimen for their mules. Seeking advice from seasoned mule farmers or veterinarians can be quite beneficial when it comes to immunization schedules, appropriate diet, and preventive care practices. Beginners may also encounter difficulties while training and managing mules, particularly if they have no prior equestrian experience. Newcomers to mule farming can gain a lot by taking the time to study appropriate training techniques and look for guidance.

FREQUENTLY ASKED QUESTIONS CONCERNING FARMING OPERATIONS AND MULE CARE

Beginners frequently have a variety of issues that need to be answered when it comes to mule care and farming activities. The longevity of mules and the length of time they may be productive on a farm are two frequently asked questions. Mules have an average lifespan of 30 to 40 years, which is longer than that of horses. When given the right attention and care, they can continue to be productive long into their senior years.

Mule breeding and reproduction is a topic that is also asked a lot.

It's a frequent misperception among beginners that mules cannot reproduce. Mules are sterile and unable to procreate in the wild. They are the progeny of a female horse named Mare and a male donkey named Jack, creating a hybrid that is incapable of having children of its own.

Other often-asked topics include the necessity for exercise, housing for mules, and handling gear. Mule care and farming operations require the provision of appropriate shelter, frequent exercise, and equipment like leads and halters.

RESOURCES FOR ADDITIONAL EDUCATION AND ASSISTANCE

There are lots of resources accessible for those who want to learn more about mule farming and need assistance. Mule farming-related online forums and groups offer a place for people to ask questions, share experiences, and get guidance from more experienced mule farmers. Books and articles about training and caring for horses frequently have parts devoted to mules, providing insightful information about their special needs and traits.

Beginners' knowledge and abilities in mule farming can also be improved by participating in training sessions, seminars, or workshops organized by mule professionals. Topics including mule handling, health care, harnessing, and driving skills are frequently covered at these gatherings. Additionally, networking possibilities, educational resources, and even mule-related events like exhibitions and competitions can be accessed by joining local or national mule associations. By using these tools, novices can gain the confidence and skill necessary to successfully negotiate the complexities of mule farming.

GETTING IN TOUCH WITH COMMUNITIES THAT FARM MULES

The support and friendship that mule farming communities provide is one of the most important resources for newcomers to the business. These communities, whether local or virtual, unite people who are enthusiastic about mules and provide a lot of information and assistance. By participating in internet forums and social media groups, novices can network with seasoned mule farmer's worldwide, exchanging advice, working through problems, and acknowledging accomplishments.

Additionally, there are possibilities for networking, mentorship, and experiential learning in the local mule farming community. Participating in local mule activities, workshops, or exhibits gives novices the chance to network with experienced farmers, pick up tips from the pros, and even present their mules. Developing ties within the mule farming community not only promotes growth and learning but also a feeling of community and a common interest in these amazing animals. Novices can start a rewarding adventure in mule farming and get useful insights and significant connections by actively participating in mule farming communities.